Printed in the United States of America

First Edition: August 2022

MICA MONOPOLY

Sai Sar

For my family

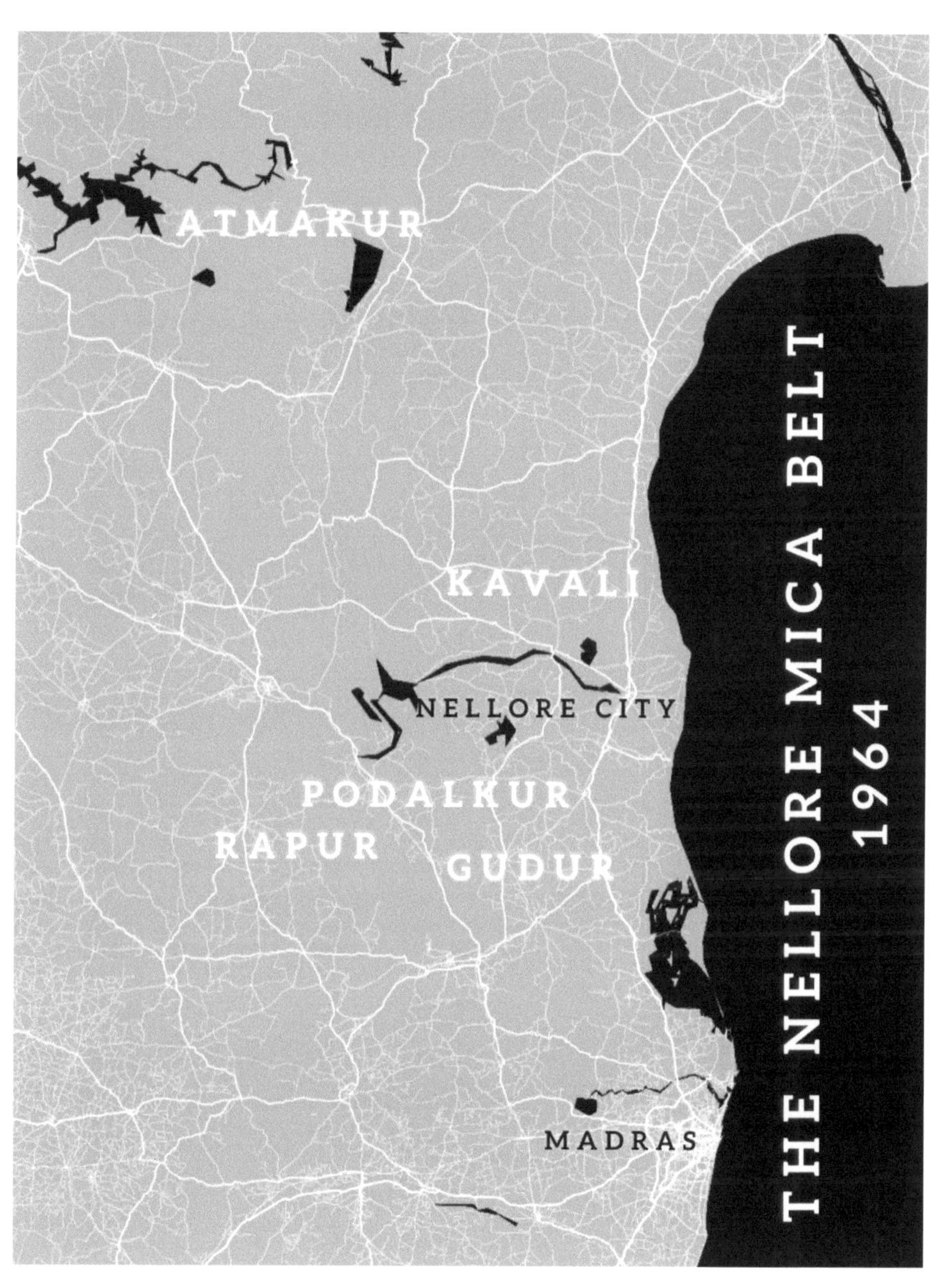

ATMAKUR
KAVALI
NELLORE CITY
PODALKUR
RAPUR
GUDUR
MADRAS
THE NELLORE MICA BELT 1964

THE BELT

Andhra Pradesh is a Telugu-speaking state in southern India, characterized by vast swaths of fertile land, a seemingly endless coastline, lush jungles, and Dravidian architecture. Being such a diverse state, it's only natural for it to produce diverse resources; some being nowhere else on earth. But of all these products, the high-quality strains of mica crystals that lie beneath were once the most sought after.

Mica is a translucent crystal, which forms in thin, plate-like clumps. These plates can be split into thin and flexible sheets, allowing them to be used in everything from electrical products to makeup. Up until the 21st century, India had a monopoly on crude mica production, responsible for the majority of global supply. But while India as a whole is frequently credited for such success, most of it was coming from the small coastal district of Nellore, where most of this substance was coming from.

While mica was common throughout the district, it was only harvested in the villages of Gudur, Raipur, Podalakur, Atmakur, and Kavali. Called the Nellore Mica Belt, each of these mining operations was run separately by individual families. Keeping mica production separate not only created unnecessary competition but decreased profits for all parties involved in the long run. But in 1964, the Kavali family began uniting the Nellore Mica Belt, building a mica monopoly.

KINGS OF KAVALI

A tall man wears a black suit, complementing his pitch-black hair, neatly combed to the side. Two men of equal height stand behind him. They look over at a roughly five-acre plot of barren land that seemed to shimmer as if it was sprinkled with glitter. All that glitters is not gold; in this case, it was mica. An arrangement of holes, anywhere from 20 to 70 feet into the ground were scattered throughout the field. A man dressed in khaki pants and a blue buttoned shirt walked up next to the men and greeted them. "Apologies for the delay, a herd of goats was blocking the road." He looks over at the field, "but it looks like you've made your way here without me," he chuckles. Just then, a small hand reaches up out of a hole in the distance. A small child, covered in silica dust and red dirt climbs out, holding a bamboo basket full of raw mica. Five more children followed her out, dropping their harvest in a pile just outside, before climbing back into the darkness.

One of them asks, "Is it safe?"

The man in the blue button shirt nervously chuckles, "Sure, sure, they're plenty safe." Truth be told, there wasn't anything remotely safe about it. The tunnels the child laborers descend into tend to collapse, trapping the miners underneath pounds of debris, until they slowly, but surely suffocate to death.

The tall man in the suit had all the reassurance he needed. He turns to the man in the blue button shirt, and announces "We'll buy it." And so, the Kavali family bought their way into the cut-throat world of mica mining. But for now, the only throats on the line are those of the child laborers.

The Kavalis had initially been a land-owning family, based in the homonymously named Kavali Administrative Division of Nellore District. During British rule, which had ended only 15 years back in 1947, they sustained their prominence by providing agricultural resources to them. Kavali Kondappa, the head of the family, had three sons with his wife Venilla; Shiva, then twins Daksh, and Billa. They later had a daughter, Kamini. As the sons grew older, so did their desire to escape their father's shadow and create a name for themselves. With Shiva acting as financier, the trio used their father's lands as collateral to qualify for loans, and partook in several business ventures - they all failed miserably. That was - until they got into mica. As suggested by a family friend, the lack of competition, increasing demand, and support from their father, the wealthiest man south of the Godavari river, giving them a headstart in the business. Their initial plot of leased land soon grew into several, eventually amalgamating into the biggest mica mine in Kavali. Of course, Kavali wasn't the only part of the district that was home to mica mining operations. At first, the brothers sold products only within India, slowly establishing contacts with distributors in other states. It wasn't until they began looking to expand internationally, that their competition began posing a problem.

The Chinese were the most frequent buyers of mica, buying in bulk and processing it for use in their products. Mica's commercial viability and the advent of the Vietnam War, which needed mica's wide range of military applications for the construction of airplanes, rockets, and guns made the demand for Indian mica surge. But although they were the most *frequent* buyers of the mineral, they only bought in small shipments; an effort to minimize loss from pirates. During this period, several bands of rogue thieves frequently attacked and stole cargo and even entire boats, in the South China Sea. Because of the ongoing wars in Southeast Asia, air travel was heavily restricted, not to mention dangerous, and therefore impractical. This left shipping as the only viable option.

The Russians on the other hand, lived inland, which meant

the only economical way to reach them was via air. Since the center of the Soviet nation was located directly northwest of India, it was free of any war-time travel restrictions. This made it possible for the Russians to buy in bulk - they *always* bought in bulk, and always in the largest shipments possible. While their purchases were inconsistent, they provided a way of getting a lot of money. Fast.

For the Kavalis, this was their first time in the international market, so the Chinese were the safest bet. But to get their product to Chinese distributors in Hong Kong, they would need a port to ship it from. Handling over 100 million metric tons of cargo per year, the port of Madras in Tamilnadu was the 2nd largest port in the country, and conveniently enough, only 4 hours south of Nellore. For the Kavali trio, it seemed like an airtight solution. Every other entrepreneur in Southern India, let alone Nellore district, had the same idea. To accommodate the increasing demand, and prevent residents from being eclipsed by competitors from other states, the port of Madras licensed only 3 consignors per state to operate. Maithreyi Transport was the only shipper of the three that went as far east as Hong Kong.

The following Monday, the brothers departed to Madras early in the morning, reaching around lunchtime. Stepping out of their white muscle car, they were immediately greeted by the smell of Madras Fish Curry. The salty ocean air washed over them, distracting them from the infamous smog and pollution that was common further inland. It was around noon, and a faint Muslim prayer was being announced in the distance. They were standing in front of a large cargo ship, *"MAITHREYI"*, printed in English on its white hull in bright red letters.

In Telugu, Kavali means "want," but for the Kavali brothers, getting this contract was a *need*. Shiva, walked in front, a dapper suit with a black briefcase in his right hand, the other falling into his left pocket. Daksh wore gold studded shades and a grey suit, maintaining an almost carefree stride, while Billa wore khaki pants and a white button shirt, which was folded up on the sides revealing his muscular composure, three buttons left open, revealing his gold chain. All three wore the same, identical thick, 18" gold chain around their neck, holding a pendant of a golden tiger head, and two bronze roses.

They were greeted by two police officers at the entrance of the ship but were turned away, as "Sir was busy," and told to come back later. Before the trio could respond in whatever broken Tamil they had picked up from the movies, a loud chopping sound was heard in the distance.

One of the officers standing guard promptly picked up his walkie-talkie and whispered, *"Mutalāḷi vantuviṭṭār;" the boss has arrived.* No sooner had the message been sent, did the asphalt pebbles on the ground begin to tremble. The loud pulsating sound only grew louder, until a green camo chopper appeared overhead. As it landed in front of them, the dust temporarily blinded the bystanders. Glitters of white, red, and gold were the only visuals they had. As the chopper flew away, and the dust settled, a tall man with a manicured beard and a salt-and-pepper slicked-back hairstyle remained. The white they had seen was his suit, the red being his undershirt. The gold sparkle was the jewelry he'd neatly adorned himself with. The man was about the same height as Shiva but towered over the twins.

The man smoothly removed his silver sunglasses and began walking towards the brothers, a slight smile hidden by his manicured beard. Putting his hands together - a sign of respect and welcome in India - Shiva walked towards the man and introduced himself, the twins following closely behind. The man in the white suit confidently removed his shades and shook his hand firmly.

Shiva introduces himself in broken Tamil *"Vaṇakkam en peyar Shiva;" Hello, my name is Shiva.*

The man in the white suit chuckles, "Alfonso, Alfonso L'Silva - English is fine by the way."

"Portuguese?" Shiva questions.

Maintaining a calm chuckle, L'Silva replies, "Indian born and raised, just Catholic." India has no official religion, so a plethora of religions, such as Hindusim, Catholicism, Islam, and

Sikhism all thrive throughout the country. Usually, Catholics are concentrated on India's west coast, as Shiva's surprise suggests.

The twins introduce themselves as well and follow L'Silva to his office inside the ship. As they sat down, Shiva was tempted to ask about how a regional businessman had access to a helicopter, since, in the 1960s, the Indian army was the only entity that had access to aircraft, let alone military-grade helicopters. But Shiva, being the straight-shooter his father had raised him to be, got straight to the point.

Shiva began to explain their background in business and their entry into the mining business, but before he could finish, L'Silva made sure to set a precedent. "Listen, I think that this is great. It's great that your business is booming, and you've amassed such knowledge in this field in such a short time - especially at your age - but at the end of the day I care about one thing, and one thing only - profit." Acknowledging the brothers' astonished expressions, he continues "Listen, I don't schedule meetings, regardless of who referred you, without running a background check first. Here's what I'll do for you. I'll take your first shipment to Hong Kong free of cost, I'll reimburse you in case of any loss - there won't be - but if need be. For any further shipments, I require 10%, no less, no more - well maybe more - of all products that make it to Hong Kong. Deal?"

Shiva, who was prepared to offer 50%, eagerly agreed. The men laughed and signed the necessary paperwork, as tea from the plantations of West Bengal up north, was set down in front of them. Now that they'd secured a shipper, they were able to send their product to Hong Kong. Being one of the only international suppliers of mica in India, let alone Nellore, they could dominate their smaller competition in Kavali. They'd become the only mining operation in the Kavali Administrative Division. They'd become the mining kings of Kavali. That was - if they could get their product to the dock in the first place.

NOTHING GOOD IN GUDUR

In the small town of Kavali, signs of the southwest monsoon were becoming ever prevalent. The days were growing shorter, the humidity was increasing, and lower temperatures were accompanied by occasional herds of stratocumulus clouds. It was October 12, 1964, and a year has passed since the brother's international debut. It was also the 9th and final day of Navratri, an annual Hindu festival that spans over nine nights, and celebrates the battle that occurred between the goddess, Durga, and the demon, Mahishasura (Ma-hi-sha-sura) - who represents the ego.

While the story varies per region, the residents of Kavali believe that the demon Mahishasura performed severe penance and meditation for years. This led to him being granted immortality by Brahma (one of three main forms of God in Hinduism) and having been told that he could only be defeated by a woman. When he began causing havoc in both heaven and hell, the holy trinity: Brahma, Vishnu, and Shiva came together and created - Durga, a warrior goddess. She fought with the buffalo-headed demon for 9 days and nights, but with each drop of his blood that touched the ground, a clone appeared. This tiresome cycle repeated, until on the 9th night of the battle, the goddess turned into her final form - Kali. While Durga, was a beautiful, tiger-mounted warrior goddess who held a weapon in each of her 8 hands, and was draped in a silk saree and adorned with heavenly gold, her reincarnation, Kali, was a far cry from her aura of perfection. Kali wore only tiger skin and a chain of skulls to cover her dark blue skin, and held nothing but a single knife in one of her 4 hands. To prevent him from respawning, she drank each drop of blood before it touched the ground. By the end of this 9th day, every drop of his blood had been consumed, and the demon had been defeated. The universe had been saved by a woman - a pattern that would soon be repeated.

Historically, it had been a tradition in the village for the leaders to host a grand Navratri festival, large enough to accommodate all the millions of local people they employed. Since the Kavali family had already made a name for themselves with their sizable agriculture holdings, well before their venture into the mining industry, they held the responsibility.

The aroma of incense, jasmine, and burning plastic filled the air. A plethora of foods - of every shape, size, and color - were being prepared, as children lit fireworks by the dozen. Nearby, young women performed traditional dances, while musicians recited traditional stories and played rhythmic songs to guide them. This bouquet of colorful celebrations was contained inside the local temple complex, which was enclosed by 4 walls, painted with red and white stripes. At the center of each of these walls, stood tall, truncated-pyramidal structures. These gatehouses, called gopurams, have thousands of colorful, intricate sculptures carved throughout them. At the very center of the square complex, was a large geometric step well, about 5 stories into the ground. The lowest two stories were engulfed by the groundwater. And at the very center of the pool, was a single, flat, sandstone slab, wide enough for a fire pit at its center. Not too long after sunset, the head priest exits the main temple, which was facing directly towards the stepwell, and blows a conch shell, signaling the population that it was time for the homam, a fire ritual is done every year to ensure prosperity for the region. The celebration came to halt as quickly as it had begun, as the villagers settled themselves on the steps surrounding the homam. The Kavali family was instructed by the 3 head priests to perform the homam. But just as the fire was lit, as the first of many

Sanskrit hymns were chanted, a flash of light flooded the sky. At first, a single drop fell from the sky on Billa's nose. Then another, and another, until the seemingly quiet drizzle exploded into a full-blown storm. The people were beginning to leave, but the head priest quickly informed the family that the ritual must be completed, or it would bring bad luck for the rest of the year.

Knowing he'd need to act fast, Billa quickly took the angavastram (shoulder cloth) portion of his dhoti (a type of sarong usually worn by men) to cover the fire. The villagers see that they are going forward with the homam, even though the thunderstorm, and sit back down to support them. The secondary priests reluctantly follow the command of their teacher and perform the homam, but as the homam comes to a close, the rain eventually seeps through the cloth and dampens the fire. The crowd grows worried as the last embers struggle to burn, until, at the very last moment, a bolt of lightning swiftly hits the very center of the pit, and the fire is revived. The priests instructed the Kavalis to complete the homam until completion, and hope is returned to the villagers.

The following morning, the sky is fairly clear, with a light blanket of fog reducing visibility, but the rains seem to have receded. The Kavali brothers take their parents' blessings, get into their white muscle car, the Premier Padmini (a popular car at the time), and tell the driver to head to the Port of Madras. Behind them followed 22 lorries, which are a type of truck popular in India for their lack of a roof, which allows for more product to be transported on a single-vehicle. The lorries follow their car, driving through miles of farmland until they arrive at the Penna Bridge; the sky clears as the day progresses. The fastest way to Madras was by cutting straight through Nellore City, but the Penna River separated the city and the northern reaches of the country for miles. While the Penna Bridge, rising 12 meters (42 feet) above sea level, was built back in 1863 to tackle this issue, its British designers had failed to account for one *very* important factor; monsoon season. The rains from the night before had caused slight disturbances for the homam back in Kavali, but down here, they had caused the penna river to flood to such a level that the bridge was no longer viable.

The only alternative was to drive west until they reached the Lankamalla Reserve - where the river is subdued by the Somasila Dam - but with weak quality of the roads and random checks from forest rangers, they'd have no chance of getting to Madras on time. But this was their first delivery for L'Silva, so setting such precedents wasn't in their best interests if they wanted to keep this deal long-term.

Billa, after stepping out to inspect the situation, was about to head back into the car, when a bright light temporarily blinds him. It was a train of lorries - around 30 of them - parking next to the brother's car. Their initial confusion quickly soured into anger, after seeing such utter disobedience from their crew, but they soon realized that they weren't their trucks at all. Instead of the family crest, the face of a tiger painted in gold, on the side of each red lorry, which was hand-painted with psychedelic designs and colors, the Kavali brand, the trucks were painted completely black, with the image of a large green crescent moon engulfing a star painted on the back of each truck. The brothers knew immediately, and so did every member of their crew behind them; the trucks belonged to the Mustafa mica mining family of Gudur.

Gudur is a small town on the *NH16*, the national highway connecting Nellore to Madras. While state surveys have consistently indicated that the district is home to a primarily Hindu population, the small town of Gudur has always been the exception, where, home to half a dozen mosques, boasts one of the largest Muslim populations anywhere in the state. India is home to every religion in the world, but Muslims and Hindus in particular, have historically always had several disagreements. When the British divided the northern regions of India based on religion, these religious tensions only grew. Eventually, these tensions resulted in a series of violent confrontations between the two groups throughout the country. Because of this, being Muslim in Hindu-majority India and starting your own business, much less attaining success, was quite rare.

The brothers mockingly chuckled under their breath, assuming the trucks would soon come to the same conclusion. They began to pull off of the river bed, but Billa noticed that the long line of lorries didn't seem to be moving. When brought to his brother's attention, he was quickly dismissed, as the brothers were deciding how to save their deal with L'Silva. But Billa still felt something was off, so he disregarded his brothers and promptly jumped out of the moving car and crept to the riverbed, hearing faint voices in the distance, only growing louder as he neared the water; and that's where he saw it. The lorries weren't moving because they were unloading their cargo. *Mustafa Mining* had managed to charter a small barge, a wide boat built to carry large vehicles, and bring it to the Penna river. Now that the river had flooded, large vessels could access the waterway.

Billa immediately rushed back and informed his brothers, who rushed to see the spectacle for themselves. It wasn't long before the brothers gave each other the same calculative look; they knew what they needed to do. Billa quietly informed each of their 22 lorries to exit the river bank and reposition themselves next to Mustafa's when they drove back in. The blue sky they were met with earlier that day was now polluted with storm clouds, and a light drizzle was rapidly evolving into something more. The sun was completely blocked out, reducing visibility to a point where the lorries could be differentiated from one another. The brothers left their car and replaced 3 of the lorry drivers. They followed the black lorries onto the barge and began loading the rest of their cargo onto the barge as well. By this time, heavy rain was pouring down, so heavy in fact that the barge operators failed to account for the surplus of vehicles, 22 to be exact, that had made their way onto the barge. Unfortunately for the brothers, while the conditions may have allowed them and their cargo passage across the Penna, it distracted them from noticing the black tarps that had been mounted on top of the black lorries.

In about 9 minutes, the barge anchored on the other side of the river, and the trucks began exiting and merging back onto the NH16. Since the highway was the fastest way to Madras, the brothers followed them in their individual lorries, as their crew of 19 followed close behind; they figured that they'd lose them at Gudur, which was most likely where they were headed.

About half an hour through the drive, the lorries begin exiting the highway. The brothers knew that if they continued driving, they'd be able to reach Madras on time, and avoid any unwanted run-ins with Mustafa's men. It was the smart thing to do; it was the most efficient, sensible, and financially productive thing to do - not to mention that it would benefit all parties involved. But Billa couldn't stop wondering why Mustafa's trucks were crossing from the north, since Gudur was down south. Whether it was due to the rains, or an act of sheer stupidity, he followed the black lorries off the highway and into the palm tree plantation. The brothers, shocked by Billa's actions, promptly pulled to the side of the road. Daksh suggested they follow Billa, but Shiva couldn't afford to sacrifice this deal. So, they agreed that Daksh would follow Billa, while Shiva would lead the rest of the 20 lorries to Madras.

The black lorries had stopped at a tea stall, where the drivers had gathered around and were enjoying a cup of tea. The sky was clearing around this time, so Billa parked his lorry a mile or so before the stalls, to avoid his lorry from being seen. As he was stepping out, Daksh pulls up behind him. He tries to reason with Billa, but Billa seems set on getting to the drivers. In all honesty, he wasn't sure what he was looking for, but he had come too far to head back. Daksh and Billa head to the tea stall, and order 2 cups for themselves. They casually lean on the edge of the straw hut, as their tea was being prepared. The drivers hadn't noticed their lorries, so they continue talking as they were. It wasn't until the brothers had finished their tea and were about to head back, did they get their answer. They overheard two of the drivers discussing how they've been looting the brothers' mines to increase their harvest. That was why they were north of the river in the first place. Upon hearing this, they start to head back to inform Shiva of the situation. Billa was about to get into his lorry when he notices the black tarps on the lorries. When Billa implores one of the drivers about it, the duo quickly realizes their grave mistake.

The issue lies in the very properties of the mineral itself. Mica is excavated in sheets, which are usually transparent to opaque in color. These sheets are resilient, reflective, refractive, lightweight, dielectric, flexible, insulating, and chemically inert - and the brothers knew it. But there was one property that the Kavali brothers failed to recollect; mica is highly hydrophilic, which means that a bare mica surface is prone to absorbing water. The mica they were transporting, all 22 truckloads of it, was not only bare but straight from the ground. It wouldn't matter how quickly they got their product to Madras if it was unusable.

The brothers looked at each other and they know what they needed to do. Billa stands on top of a large tire, and speaks to the crows of about 30 drivers. He attempts to bribe them and asks them to sell him the mica. Assuming that they weren't aware of its worth, he offers an amount less than 20% of a single lorry's load - for all 30 trucks. The men saw the brothers' high-end clothes and gold jewelry and were immediately incentivized to take the deal. Unfortunately for Billa, an elderly man sat up from the crowd. He had a long white beard and used the branch of a sugar apple tree to stand. He wore the same khaki uniform as the rest of the drivers.

He faced the rest of the drivers and spoke as loud as he could, with the little energy he had left in his frail body.

"I have worked for Mustafa for almost 20 years. Like many of you, I used to be a farmer, year in and year out, I depended on the seasonal rains and so did the rest of my family. Back then, locusts had been plaguing the state, and I had lost my entire crop. I couldn't feed my family or send my children to school. I had decided that if I couldn't support my family, there was no point in me being alive. So, I decided to drink the pesticide - listen I don't know how well it worked on the bugs, but it worked fine on me. I was on the floor convulsing in less than a minute. I was taken to the local hospital, where it was Mustafa who offered me the job. I owe my life to him. I'm too old to tell you all what to do, but whatever money they're offering isn't going to buy my loyalty -

not mine."

Almost as quickly as they'd agreed to the bribe, the crowd exploded into commotion. One of the men sees the gold tiger pendant on Daksh's gold chain. He points it out, realizing that they were connected with the Kavali family. The band of drivers, feeling somewhat guilty for considering the bribe, decide to take the competitors directly to their boss. Daksh tries resisting the men at first, but after seeing Billa's submissive stance, also decides to surrender. They are taken to separate lorries and tied to the seats; if only the drivers knew they weren't just detaining two men, but sealing their fates.

It hasn't been more than 10 minutes after the sun disappeared into the horizon, that Billa, sitting in the first lorry, notices that the driver exits the highway onto the Old Madras Culcutta road. By this time, the sun had disappeared behind the horizon, leaving the lorries' low beams as the sole source of light. It wasn't for another mile or so until they passed two cream-colored minarets of a local mosque, almost as if to scream that the twins weren't in Kavali any longer; they were in Gudur now.

The lorries stop in front of two large black gates, where a local police officer is standing guard. The driver notifies the guard of their situation, compelling the guard to take a look for himself. Upon seeing the prisoners, his doubtful curiosity quickly melts into a panic. He quickly rushes to the gate and lets the two lorries in. The first driver parks, and warns Billa not to try anything stupid, quickly exiting the vehicle and signaling the driver behind him to follow him inside the house, painted white and built in a colonial style.

Daksh looks around the lorry, hoping to find something - someone - that could free him from his predicament. There weren't any knives, daggers, or scissors handy - even *if* there were, he wouldn't be able to reach them anyhow. He tries struggling out of the loose and grainy threads he was imprisoned with, knowing deep down it wouldn't matter. But for him, it wasn't just about escaping anymore. His futile battle with the rope was merely a distraction; a distraction from the pure frustration that boiled every neuron in his brain, making his heart pump faster, almost eliminating any blinking sensation. Not only had he lost his freedom, and possibly an international shipping contract, but a brother; he felt like he'd lost his twin. Make no mistake about it, Billa was still alive and kicking in the lorry ahead, but the mindless decisions that he'd seem to have made - left Daksh feeling isolated and alone. Since they were children, Billa had always "zoned out" at random and acted like one does when sleepwalking; usually, he snapped out of it in a few minutes so they didn't pay too much attention to it; it'd been 10 minutes now and Billa, although his eyes were wide open, wasn't responding to Daksh. At this point, Daksh was ready to give up, he'd found no options, no way to escape. So he fell back against his seat in surrender and looked up at the roof of the lorry waiting for the inevitable. That's when he realized; while he couldn't access any knives or daggers at the moment, he realized that he could access the largest weapon of them all - he was tied to it. Lorries are usually around 20 tons but are filled to the brim with raw mica, it could easily measure 40 tons (80,000 lbs). He looked around and found that the edge of the door had a sharp metal edge. He tries leaning his hands towards it, reaches it, and tries to saw the tie on his hands off. Unfortunately, it was at this moment that the two drivers returned from the house, only this time, with guns.

The drivers untied the men and took them inside the house. It was dark inside, and only a single light illuminated the living room. A man with a pruned beard and curly black hair sat alone, he was wearing a white thobe (an ankle-length robe worn by Muslims) and had kohl, a black eyeliner common for Muslim men, around his eyelid. He held a Quran in his hands, which he kept closed, but intensely stared at its front cover. Them drivers sat the two Kavalis on the sofa in front of the man, untied them, and stepped back into the shadows.

Opening the book gently, the man slowly looks up at the brothers and reads,

"'As for the male and female thieves, cut off their hands for what they have done—a deterrent from Allah.' He grabs a machete from under the sofa, startling, the twins - the drivers quickly emerge from the shadows and hold the brothers down.

"The Quran tells us that this is the way to deal with thieves." He stops and sets the machete down next to him, calming the brothers down as well, the henchmen-turned-drivers loosening their grip as well.

"You tried to steal, which makes you thieves, but the issue, you see - is that you tried to steal from me - making you my enemy. But for enemies, the Quran states "And the recompense of evil is punishment like it, but whoever forgives and amends, he shall have his reward from Allah. Ash Shuraa (42:39-42); It's telling me to forgive my enemies. As you know, I am Muslim, and I am proud. But in this country, it makes it harder for people like me to come up. You both would never know, born into the wealthiest household in the state, but that doesn't matter. What does matter is that to get where I am, and to have stayed here for so long, I can't seem weak, I just can't? Religion aside, it just isn't something I can afford."

"So tell me, Mr. Daksh and Mr. Billa, what should I see you as, an enemy or a thief?" Billa, still not in the right state of mind - if any state at all - stares blankly at him. Daksh, on the other hand, was fully in the moment, and begs him for mercy."

"Sir - please-"

"Call me Mustafa - please," the man interrupts.

"Mustafa," Daksh continues, "we were only trying to -" Daksh suddenly stops talking. He freezes in place and lets the droplets of blood roll down from his eyes into his mouth. He comes back to his senses when Billa's cleanly sliced head plummets onto his lap and rolls down to his feet. Mustafa had executed Billa. After a moment of silence, before Daksh could respond, Mustafa bared his teeth, and smiled - smiled so widely - you could see the joy in his face as Billa's splattered blood dripped from his smile - so wide in fact, it brought into question Mustafa's mental state. He stops abruptly and asks the drivers to take the men to their rooms, as they were his guests. The drivers, themselves somewhat terrified, pick up Billa's head and body and lead Daksh into a room.

During this time the state of Andhra Pradesh, like the rest of India, rationed its electricity by providing it to different parts of each district at different times. It was half-past 8 pm now, which meant Gudur would not have electricity till' the next morning. A small candle, not more than a few inches in height, was provided, and the doors were kept unlocked.

For Daksh, at least, this entire day had felt like nothing more than a fever dream. All his life, he'd looked to his brother for guidance, but although he was physically there, his emotional absence left Daksh feeling lost. He was Hansel *and* Gretal, and his breadcrumbs, the only way out of the forest were gone. He grabbed his brother's severed head and put it up against his forehead. He wanted to cry, he wanted to scream, he wanted to punch, kick, and shoot. He wanted to burn the whole world down. And that's exactly what he did.

It was the next morning, and Daksh awoke to a small creaking sound. It came from a light breeze, which passed through a pair of green, wooden windows. They were beautiful windows. It was too dark the night before, but now that the sun was shining down upon them, Daksh could appreciate them in all their glory. The workmanship was on par with those of the tribal peoples further north in Orissa, and the green paint was made using only the finest local materials.

That pair of green, wooden windows were hanging onto a slab of charred brick that used to make up one of the four walls he was sent to the night before. That pair of green wooden windows was all that was left. Billa had taken the small candle he was given and placed it next to the single lightbulb, in front of which his brother had been martyred. The lightbulb burst from the heat, and the flame from that small, wax candle, caught onto the small power generator it was attached. It immediately burst into flames, and consumed the house, with Mustafa still inside it.

Daksh stared at the ruins for a moment longer, before he picked up his brother's head, and began walking back to the main highway. He's almost at the town line when he comes upon the mosque he'd passed the night before. In Islam, Muslims are asked to pray 5 times a day. Mustafa's drivers were walking out of the mosque when they saw him with his brother's head in one hand and Mustafa's machete in the other. They knew what had happened. These drivers, who were oh so loyal to their former boss the night before, fell to their knees, asking for forgiveness. 3 hours later, Daksh and his new employees had arrived with 30 tracks of raw, viable mica at Madras Port.

These brothers may have set out to make a name for themselves, but have ruined that of another, maybe even themselves, in the process. This wasn't just a small mica mining operation any longer, it was a full-blown mica mafia.

Upon delivering the new supply of undamaged cargo, Daksh and Shiva return to Kavali with their brother's head. The Kavali household was a large building with intricate designs carved into everything from the wooden doors to the wooden pillars erected throughout the dwelling. At the center of the home, a spacious central courtyard opened up to the sky. Just beside the lily pond, at the center of this composition, was Kondappa, the brothers' father. He was reading the morning paper, waiting for his daily cup of tea, when his sons walked in with Billa's severed head. As if on cue, their mother, Venilla, sends a maid to give Kondappa his tea. The copper platter dropped to the floor faster than Billa's head. Upon hearing the commotion, Venilla rushed out of the kitchen. Kondappa was frozen, still staring at his two sons, and what used to be part of his third. The brothers, half expecting the depths of hell to open up under their feet were surprised to see their mother's reaction. She wasn't screaming, yelling, or bursting into tears. Instead, she seemed focused, as if starting an exam she had never studied for.

"What happened," she asked.

Shiva explained the situation, as he had heard from Daksh. Daksh proudly stated that he had burned Mustafa alive in his own home. They were shocked to hear her answer.

"I never thought I'd say this, but I'm disappointed. That death was too easy for that bottom feeder. You should have brought him to me - alive. I'd feed his eyes to the dogs, right after I peel his skin off his body with my bare hands and stuff it down his throat. Then, and only then, would I even *think* of wasting a single match on that animal." She wasn't going to have her son's death be in vain. She had Shiva and Daksh promise to complete whatever it was that Billa had started.

They began funeral preparations for Billa the next morning. Well, at least what was left of him. The males of the family gathered around a funeral pyre on the banks of the Krishna river, all dressed in customary white. Unlike the dry banks of the Penna that ultimately led to his death, the lush jungles around the Krishna would guide his soul to its next destination.

Kondappa, the brothers' father and head of the Kavali household, was known throughout the district for his strength, courage, and bravery. Yet, today, his eyes seemed frail and tired, as if he hadn't slept for days. Shiva, although trying to mirror his father's brooding nature, couldn't prevent a few tears from sliding down his cleanly shaven face. Daksh, on the other hand, looked different, he felt different - he was different. It wasn't sadness, pity, or mourning, but anger. Angry at his brother for leaving him when he needed him most, angry at Mustafa for killing him, and most of all, angry at himself for letting it happen. He glared intensely at the fire, almost as if wanting it to consume him instead of what used to be his brother. That youthful disposition he was once associated with had died off with his brother. It may have been because of his carefree attitude, or his colorful attire, that Daksh was always considered the youngest in the family. But in reality, it was his sister Kamini, now a prominent lawyer in London, who claimed that title.

The priest initiating the rites suddenly stops. A faint whirring sound in the distance breaks the sanctity of the scene. A white helicopter lands in the distance, just far enough so the funeral pyre isn't disturbed. A lady in a navy blue sheath dress - popular in 1960s London - white high heels, pearl earrings, and pearl necklace steps out onto the red dirt, holding her neatly wrapped bun in the process. She takes off her white gloves and waves the helicopter goodbye, making her way to the pyre; it was the brothers' sister and the youngest in the family - Kamini. She walks up to her father Kondappa and kisses his cheek. He caresses her face, whispering "it's good to have you back." Kondappa requests the priest to continue with the rituals, almost as if he had expected her to come. Shiva immediately embraces her, but Daksh is still turned to the fire.

She takes off her sunglasses and faces the pyre. "I return after so long, not a hug, or a nod."

He quickly responds, "Kamini, you do something useful, I'll nod my head for as long as you want." Their father glares at Daksh, instantly settling him down.

She responds "This is our brother's funeral, this isn't the time or the place"

He snarkily rebuffs, "It never quite is with you, is it?" Daksh looks over at Kamini and sees that she is wearing blue, as opposed to the customary white. "Figures."

"What?"

Referring to her outfit, "Even today, you can't put yourself aside."

Kamini sighs, frankly quite disappointed at her brother's disillusionment responds,

"blue was his favorite color." Seeing Daksh's silence as a victory, she continues, "Mom called me and told me the news. I don't know what happened, or how, quite frankly I don't care. But I promised her, as I'm told you did too, that his death wouldn't be in vain."

"Yeah, and what are you going to do about it.

"No brother, what are *We* going to do about it."
Slightly intrigued, Shiva turned to her as well. "Mustafa is already dead, and we have his business now."

"You always thought too small brother. What is just Mustafa's business going to do? By the time we are done, we'll have every mica mine in the district under our control. And that's a promise."

Regardless of how they felt about her, the brothers knew

the value of her word. The only question was if they'd keep theirs.